I0766991

Making a decision to have
a child... it is to decide
forever to have your heart go
walking around outside
your body.

Elizabeth Stow

Date

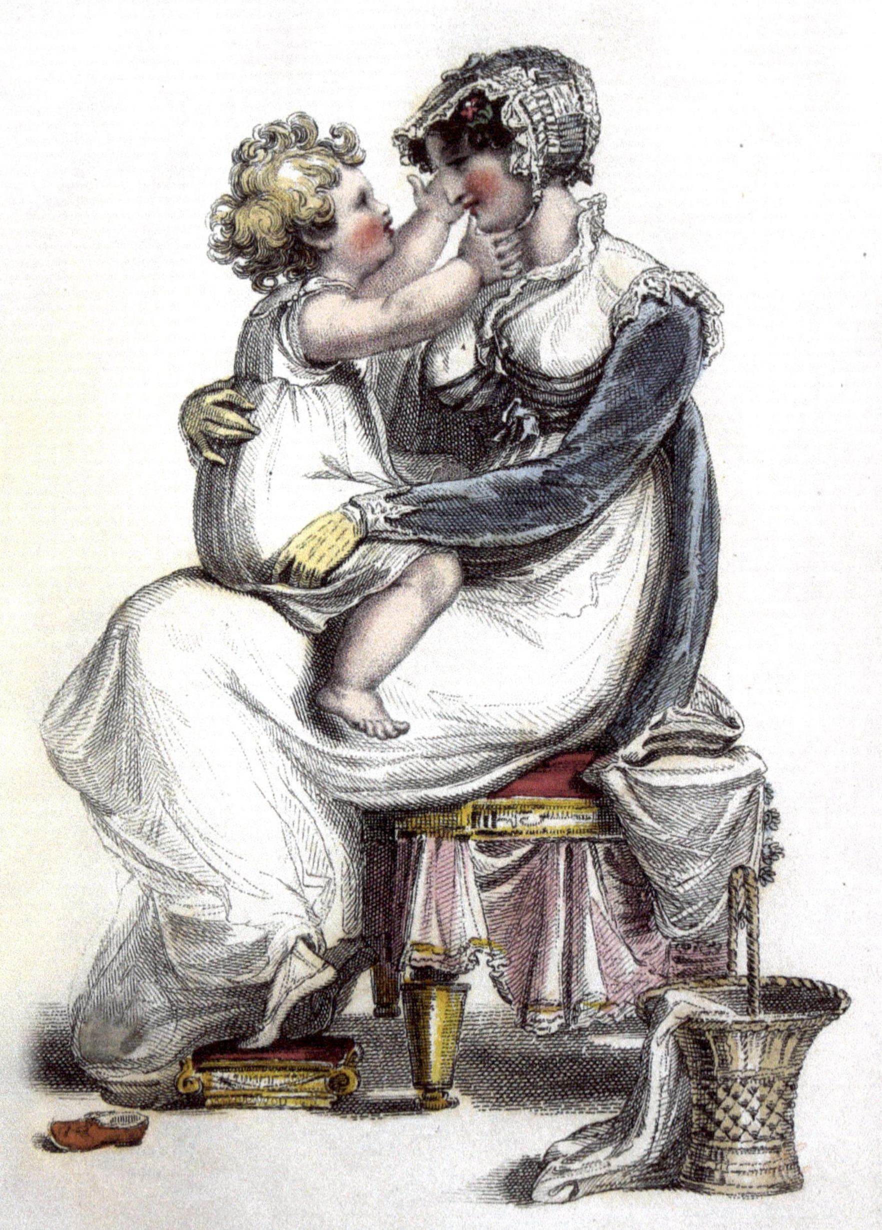

Date

Date

Date

Date

Date

Date

Date

1833

Date

Date

Date

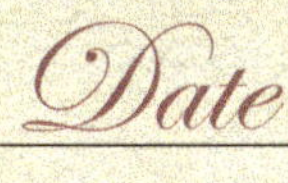

Date

Date

Date

Jules David

Date

Laure Noël

Date

Laure Noël.
Barreau
Grognet, Imp.r de Fleuve, 30

Date

Date

Gilquin fils, imp. Paris

Date

Date

Leroy, imp. Paris

Date

Date

Leroy imp. r. des Marais, 66.
A. Goubaud et fils Ed.rs Paris
1005.B.

Date

Imp. Lamoureux, Paris.
182

Date

Lumière, imp. r. du Sabot, 3.
Ad. Goubaud & Fils Edr Paris
PREVAL
1018 B

Date

Imp. Lamoureux. Paris.

Date

Leroy imp. Paris

Date

Gilquin. imp. Paris

Date

Date

Gibout imp Paris

Date

Th. DUPUY, 22 R DES PETITS HÔTELS. PARIS

Date

Date

Date

Date

25.e année
Falconer, imp. à Paris

Date

Date

Date

Date

Date

Date

Date

IMP. TH. DUPUY & FILS, RUE DES PETITS-HOTELS, 31, PARIS.
4118

Date

Jules David
Larivière imp. r du Cherche Midi. 13.
1796
N° 15. 1881

Date

A. Le Roy Imp. rue des Marais 66

Date

Larivière imp. r. du Cherche-Midi. 79.

Date

Date

A. Leroy imp. r. des Marais 66.

Date

Jules David
Lacroivière imp. r. du Cherche-Midi 79.
N° 9
AD. Goubaud & Fils, Édrs.

Date

Date

1645
A. Leroy imp. r. des Marais 66.

Date

PRIX DES PLACES
BALCON
FAUTEUIL
AMPHITHEATRE
Jules David
A. Leroy imp. r. des Marais 66.
A. Bodier
1654
Ad. Goubaud & Fils Edit. Paris

Date

A. Leroy imp. r des Marais 66

Jules David
Leroy imp. r. des Marais 66.

Date

Date

Larivière imp. r. du Cherche-Midi. 59.

Date

Date

Date

Jules David
A. Bodin 2352 E
Paris. Ap. Goubaux imp.
Reproduction interdite
Abel Goubaud, édit. Paris
No 13. 1887

Reproduction interdite

Jules Barré
E. Gaillard
Lavioère imp. Paris
Reproduction interdite
N° 35. 1887
Abel Goubaud Ed. Paris

Date

Falconer, imp. Paris.
Reproduction interdite
Abel Goubaud Edit. Paris
Nº 44 1887

Date

Paris Mr Godchaux impr Système Guy Bté S.G.D.G.
Reproduction interdite

Date

Jules David
1861°
Lariviere imp. r. du Cherche-Midi 79.
Ad. Goubaud & Fils Ed.rs Paris
N° 51_1881

Date

Carmier imp. Paris.
Reproduction interdite

Date

Date

Reproduction interdite

Date

Date

Esnault
Imp. Falconer. Paris
475

Date

Date

Lariviere imp. r.du Cherche-Midi. 29.

Date

Date

Jules David
Lamere Imp. Paris
Reproduction interdite

Date

Jules David
Th. Reforre, imp. Paris
Reproduction interdite

Date

Imp. Edelmann Paris
Sortier
Arnould

Date

H. Lefèvre. Imp. Paris
Reproduction interdite
Nº 7 - 1891.
Abel Goubaud. Edr. Paris

Date

Date

Hardcover ISBN 978-1-7750654-1-8

Summary: Memory journal dedicated to all mothers and their ethernal bond with their
children. Featuring 80 full colour fashion plates from various French, Brithish and Italian
fashion periodicals published between year 1800 and 1900.